Buying Distressed or Underperforming Online Businesses

How to Turn Around Struggling Digital Businesses for Huge Upside

By Joe Correa

Published by Live Stronger Faster

This book is for educational and informational purposes only. The author and publisher are not engaged in rendering legal, financial, or other professional advice. Readers should consult a qualified professional before making any financial decisions.

First Edition

Table of Contents

Have you ever wanted to buy an online business 5

Chapter 1: Why Distressed Businesses Are Hidden Gems 7

Chapter 2: Where to Find Distressed or Underperforming Online Businesses 15

Chapter 3: Why Due Diligence Matters Most in Distressed Deals 23

Chapter 4: The 80/20 Rule of Turnarounds 31

Chapter 5: Why You Have Leverage in Distressed Deals 39

Chapter 6: Why Traffic Is the Lifeline of Your Turnaround 46

Chapter 7: Why Systems Are the Difference Between a Job and an Asset 54

Chapter 8: Know Your Endgame Before You Begin 63

Chapter 9: From a Single Deal to a Portfolio of Profit Machines 70

Closing Thoughts 77

Have you ever wanted to buy an online business

Have you ever wanted to buy an online business — but didn't want to pay full price for something already thriving? What if you could pick up a digital asset for pennies on the dollar, fix just a few key problems, and turn it into a profitable machine?

That's exactly what this book is about.

Whether you're looking at neglected content sites, under-monetized e-commerce stores, or SaaS tools with great potential but poor execution — there are *goldmine opportunities* in the world of distressed or underperforming online businesses.

Inside this book, you'll learn:

- Why these businesses are often easier to improve than you think
- Where to find them and how to evaluate hidden potential
- The top 10 signs of an opportunity worth pursuing
- How to negotiate and structure smart deals

- Tactical turnaround strategies that create immediate wins
- And how to build systems that increase value — fast

I'll also walk you through real-world examples, deal breakdowns, and turnaround frameworks I've personally used to take struggling sites and turn them into profitable, scalable assets.

Whether you're brand new to online business or an experienced investor looking to expand your portfolio, this guide will equip you with a proven game plan to buy low, improve fast, and grow big.

Let's get started.

Chapter 1: Why Distressed Businesses Are Hidden Gems

What Is a "Distressed" or "Underperforming" Business?

In the online business world, a **distressed business** is one that's operating far below its potential — often due to neglect, poor management, outdated content, bad marketing, or a lack of monetization strategy. It's not necessarily a "bad" business — just a **mismanaged** or **underutilized** one.

Key traits of a distressed or underperforming online business:

- Traffic has declined or stagnated
- Revenue is inconsistent or flat
- Owner is disengaged or wants out
- Outdated tech, SEO, or content
- Poor customer experience or abandoned email list
- No reinvestment in growth or innovation

These traits may scare off the average buyer — but for you, they represent a massive opportunity.

The Asymmetry of Opportunity

The beauty of buying distressed online businesses lies in the **asymmetric upside**.

You're acquiring something that others overlook — usually at a steep discount — and applying simple but high-leverage improvements.

For example:

- A $15,000 content site with outdated SEO and no email capture can often double in value with just 30–60 days of optimization.
- A $10/month SaaS tool with a 5% churn rate and poor onboarding might be worth $20/month per user once properly tuned — instantly doubling MRR.

That means you can buy low, improve fast, and potentially **flip the business for 2–5x ROI** in under a year — or keep it for cash flow.

Why These Deals Are Everywhere (But Few Touch Them)

Here's the truth: distressed online businesses are **everywhere**.

They show up on:

- Flippa

- Empire Flippers (lower-tier listings)
- Acquire.com
- MicroAcquire's hidden listings
- IndieHackers and subreddits
- Cold outreach to niche creators

Many business owners simply don't have the time, tech skills, or marketing knowledge to fix what's broken. Others are just tired and want out.

Yet most buyers skip these listings, thinking:

> "Too much work... too risky... I want something already making $5K/month."

This is where the **gold is buried**.

If you have the frameworks and playbook to identify **fixable problems**, you'll see deals others miss.

The Psychology of Sellers

Most sellers of distressed businesses are **not greedy**. In fact, they're often relieved someone wants their project.

Many are:

- Solo founders burned out or starting a new job
- Creators with no monetization strategy
- Owners facing life changes (divorce, kids, etc.)
- People who built something but lost motivation

They're not looking for a massive exit — just a **clean break**.

This means you can negotiate:

- Creative payment structures
- Low upfront cash offers
- Seller financing
- Earn-outs tied to performance

And because you're solving a **problem** for them (unloading a burden), they're often open to better terms than you'd get on a "hot" listing.

The Real Reasons These Businesses Struggle (And How to Spot Fixable Ones)

Here are the most **common reasons** distressed online businesses underperform — and whether they're worth fixing:

Problem	Fixable?	Example Fix
SEO is outdated or nonexistent	✅	Update keywords, add schema, fix structure
Poor conversion funnel	✅	Add opt-ins, improve CTAs, test offers
Owner doesn't run ads	✅	Launch Google/Facebook/YouTube campaigns
Tech is broken or buggy	⚠️	Only pursue if you have dev skills or a partner
Customer support failing	✅	Add VA or build help desk
Business has negative reviews	⚠️	Depends on volume; tread carefully
Legal/IP issues	❌	Avoid unless you're a pro negotiator or attorney

Your goal is to **identify leverage points**. If the core asset (content, brand, product, audience) is strong, and the issues are operational — you can fix them fast.

"The $1,200 Blog That Paid Me $60,000"

Two years ago, I was scrolling Flippa on a Friday night while sipping tea. Most of the listings were overpriced or had vague numbers. But then I saw it:

> "Niche health blog – 10,000 visits/mo – neglected – $1,200 BIN."

I clicked in. It had:

- 10,000 pageviews/month from organic traffic
- A five-year domain with a decent backlink profile
- Zero monetization
- No email list
- No updates in over a year

I reached out. The seller replied within an hour:

> "I'm just done with it. Haven't logged in in months. I'd take $1,000 if you pay today."

I wired the money that night.

Over the next 30 days, I did four things:

1. **Added display ads via Ezoic** This immediately generated $3–$5/day.

2. **Created 3 simple digital products** Guides and templates for $9–$29 each. I used ChatGPT to outline and format them.

3. **Added opt-in forms and an email automation** In the first month, I collected 280 emails.

4. **Updated 10 articles with better keywords and formatting** Traffic jumped from 10,000 to 13,000/mo within 60 days.

Within 90 days, that $1,000 investment was producing over **$900/month** in passive income.

Then came the best part: I sold it.

At month six, I listed it for $14,000 on Empire Flippers.

It sold in two weeks for $15,500.

That's a **15.5x return** in under six months. And I still use the email list to promote other products to this day.

Here's what I learned:

- Most people overlook neglected businesses
- Fixing small things has a compounding effect
- Cash flow is cool, but so is flipping

- A good domain and existing traffic are worth more than most people think

That one deal taught me how to **see opportunity where others see junk** – and I've done it over and over again since.

Chapter 2: Where to Find Distressed or Underperforming Online Businesses

Not all deals are found on public marketplaces — and the best ones usually aren't. That said, here's where to look:

1. Online Marketplaces

These are fast, easy, and beginner-friendly:

- **Flippa** – Most distressed deals under $10K live here. Filter by revenue, traffic, and "neglected" keyword mentions.
- **Acquire.com (MicroAcquire)** – A mix of SaaS, content, and ecom. Use filters to find "low revenue" or "under $50K" listings.
- **Empire Flippers** – Usually higher-priced, but the bottom tier ($20K–$80K) often has great underperformers.
- **SideProjectors / IndieMaker** – Small niche sites sold by hobbyists or devs who lost interest.

2. Facebook Groups & Subreddits

- **Groups** like "SaaS Founders", "Buy/Sell Websites", or

"Digital Assets Marketplace" often include off-market gems.

- **Subreddits** like r/EntrepreneurRideAlong, r/IndieHackers, and r/SideProject showcase projects creators are done with.

3. Cold Outreach

Send direct messages to site owners, YouTubers, or creators who:

- Haven't posted in a while
- Don't have monetization
- Have traffic or an audience Use a subject like "Interested in acquiring your site/channel" and keep it short and friendly.

What to Look For: The Ideal Distressed Deal Checklist

When evaluating potential acquisitions, ask yourself:

Is it underperforming because of...

- **Operational neglect?** (No updates, slow site, missing integrations)

- **Marketing failure?** (No paid ads, no SEO strategy, poor copy)
- **Owner fatigue?** (No support, missed emails, disengaged)
- **Outdated monetization?** (No digital products, no upsells, poor pricing)

If **yes** to any of these, the deal might be perfect — **if** there's also:

- Existing traffic (at least 1,000 visitors/month)
- Real product or content value (not spun garbage or dropship junk)
- Room to improve monetization (ads, products, offers, email)

This is what we call a **"high-leverage fix" opportunity.**

Red Flags to Avoid

Avoid buying a "fixer-upper" that's actually broken at the foundation.

Watch out for:

- **Fake traffic or blackhat SEO**

- **Suspended ad accounts or PayPal bans**
- **Massive churn in SaaS with no support system**
- **Legal risks (copyrighted content, scraped blogs, or plagiarized courses)**
- **Heavy tech debt (custom-coded, undocumented projects)**

If a project requires more effort than you or your team can fix in 30–60 days — pass. This is about quick turnarounds, not full rebuilds.

Deal Flow: How to See 100+ Listings a Month

To consistently spot deals, set up a **deal flow system**:

- **Daily alerts** on Flippa, Empire Flippers, and Acquire.com with keywords like:
    - "neglected"
    - "underperforming"
    - "no monetization"
    - "low traffic"

- Join and monitor **3–5 Facebook groups** where creators sell side projects.
- Dedicate 1–2 hours per week to **outreach emails and DMs.**
- Track all leads in a **simple Airtable/Notion CRM** with columns like:
- Niche
- Traffic
- Revenue
- Asking price
- Monetization gaps
- Turnaround plan

Within 4–6 weeks, you'll start seeing patterns — and deals that 99% of people ignore.

The 3-Minute First Filter Test

Here's how to decide whether a deal is worth digging into further:

The 3-Minute Test:

1. Does it have **existing traffic or audience**?
2. Is the product/content **decent quality**?
3. Can you spot **at least 3 easy wins** (better offer, email list, SEO update, etc.)?
4. Is the seller **motivated but reasonable**?
5. Could you fix and monetize in **under 60 days**?

If all 5 are YES, go deeper. If not, move on.

Distressed deals are **volume-based hunting** – but once you spot a good one, the upside is enormous.

"The SEO Agency That Gave Up"

Last year, I found a listing buried at the bottom of Flippa:

> "Small SEO blog with expired ads, zero email list, built in 2018. Asking $3,500 or best offer."

I almost skipped it.

But then I noticed:

- The blog had **22 evergreen SEO tutorials**
- It was ranking for **dozens of keywords** (low volume but high intent)

- The site hadn't been touched in **3 years**
- The seller was a former agency owner who had taken a full-time job and wanted to move on

I emailed him directly and asked, "What happened?"

His reply:

> "Honestly, I got tired. It was making $200/month with affiliate links back in 2020 but dropped off when Google hit me. Haven't updated it since."

We got on a Zoom call the next day.

I offered $2,200 — all cash, close in 48 hours.

He accepted.

The turnaround was simple:

- I **rewrote the top 10 blog posts** using updated SEO structure (ChatGPT helped here)
- I added a **free SEO checklist opt-in** with an email automation funnel
- I launched a $39 "SEO Mini Course" on Gumroad and embedded it in 5 articles

- I signed up for **3 new affiliate programs** with better commissions
- I plugged in **Ezoic ads**

Within 45 days, it was:

- Doing **$380/month** in affiliate + product sales
- Getting **50 email subscribers/month**
- Earning **$3/day** in ad revenue

But I didn't sell this one.

Instead, I turned it into a **lead gen engine** for SEO consulting gigs.

Today, that $2,200 site brings me in **over $1,500/month** – and I've only touched it 3 times this year.

Moral of the story?

- The deals are out there – but **you need to go looking**
- Most sellers want **freedom**, not profit
- If you can spot a few quick wins, you can **change the value of a business** in 30 days flat

Chapter 3: Why Due Diligence Matters Most in Distressed Deals

Distressed or underperforming online businesses often have **incomplete data**, emotional sellers, or confusing histories — and that makes **due diligence** even more critical.

While other buyers look for clean books and steady income, your job is to dig into the **raw potential** hidden behind the mess.

The goal isn't perfection. It's clarity:

- Where is this business *now*?
- Where can it *go*?
- What will it take to *get there*?

The Three Buckets of Due Diligence

When analyzing a deal, break your evaluation into **three key buckets**:

1. Traffic

- **Volume** – How many unique visitors/month?
- **Sources** – Organic, direct, paid, referral, social?

- **Top pages** – What content or products are driving most of the visits?

- **Search rankings** – Use tools like Ubersuggest, Ahrefs, or SEMrush to see if SEO traffic is decaying or rising.

- **Email list** – How many subscribers? What's the open/click rate?

Look for *consistent or historically high traffic* that's been neglected but has signs of life.

2. Revenue

- **How is money made?** Ads, affiliate links, digital products, subscriptions, etc.

- **Last 6–12 months** of monthly income (ideally verifiable via screenshots or dashboard access)

- **Conversion rate** – Traffic vs. sales or opt-ins

- **Abandoned monetization** – Is there a product or offer that's not being pushed?

The best deals often have **decent traffic but poor monetization** — a huge opportunity.

3. Operations

- **Who runs the site?** Solo founder, small team, freelancers?
- **Time required per week?** (Many distressed sellers do nothing, which is fine — just be honest about what *you'll* need to do.)
- **Tools & integrations** – Are they using outdated tech?
- **Broken systems** – Dead links, abandoned emails, slow load times?

If you can solve **operational gaps** in under 2–4 hours/week, it's a strong buy signal.

The Traffic–Revenue Gap Rule

One of the fastest ways to spot potential is to ask:

"Does the traffic justify more revenue?"

Here's a simple test:

Monthly Traffic	**Revenue Benchmark**	**Fixable?**
5,000 visitors	Under $100/month	Yes — add affiliate links, lead magnets, low-ticket offers
10,000+ visitors	Under $500/month	Yes — test ads, product bundles, email automation
20,000+ visitors	Under $1,000/month	Big upside — low monetization is your leverage

Tools to Analyze a Business Quickly

Here are a few tools that give you a quick, pro-level look under the hood:

- **Google Analytics or Plausible** – Actual traffic sources and engagement
- **Ubersuggest or Ahrefs** – Keyword rankings and backlink profiles
- **BuiltWith** – What tech stack is being used
- **Wayback Machine** – How the site looked in the past (to see if traffic dips match major changes)

- **Hunter.io + WHOIS** – Owner data for cold outreach (off-market deals)
- **Stripe/PayPal screenshots** – Revenue validation

If a seller doesn't have these? That's okay — ask for access, screen shares, or export reports.

The 15-Minute Quick Valuation Method

Here's a basic formula I use when evaluating underperforming businesses:

diff

CopyEdit

Adjusted Monthly Profit × 12 = Baseline Value

+ Monetization Upside = Target ROI Potential

Example:

- Site makes $200/month with 10K visitors
- You estimate that proper monetization would bump that to $800/month in 60 days
- Baseline value: $2,400
- Potential value: $9,600

Offer around $2K–$3K — you'll be getting a business you can 4x in under 3 months.

"The Mystery YouTube Channel with No Monetization"

One day, I received an odd message from a content creator I'd chatted with months earlier.

> "Hey, I'm shutting down my YouTube channel if no one buys it. You interested?"

I asked for the link. It had:

- 2,800 subscribers
- 40+ evergreen videos in the personal finance niche
- 4,500–6,000 views/month
- No monetization. Zero links. No description. Just videos.

He hadn't uploaded in over a year. I offered $750 — and he agreed.

But here's where the real due diligence began:

I plugged the channel URL into **TubeBuddy** and found:

- Multiple videos still ranking in search

- Strong average watch times (3+ minutes)
- One video was responsible for 45% of the total views

Then I looked up:

- Similar keywords on YouTube Search
- Affiliate programs in the niche (there were 5 solid options)
- A matching domain name (I bought it for $12)

I realized: this channel was a **sleeping giant**.

My turnaround plan:

1. Created a **basic landing page** with an email opt-in and affiliate links
2. Updated video descriptions and pinned comments with links
3. Added an intro/outro using Canva and InVideo
4. Recorded 5 new videos using the same style and AI voiceover
5. Scheduled videos weekly to revive the algorithm push

Result:

- Within 60 days, I had 1,200 visits/month to my landing page
- My affiliate dashboard showed $380 in commissions
- One video went semi-viral again, hitting 10K views

The best part?

I hadn't even shown my face — or recorded a voice.

It was all faceless, repurposed, and systematic.

That one $750 deal now earns me **$300–$500/month** passively — and is part of a new bundle I'll eventually flip.

The lesson?

> "If you analyze correctly, you can *see value others miss.*"

And when you do, the numbers don't lie.

Chapter 4: The 80/20 Rule of Turnarounds

When it comes to fixing a distressed digital business, **80% of the upside** often comes from just **20% of the actions**.

In most cases, the problem isn't that the business *can't* succeed — it's that the owner:

- Built it but never optimized
- Started strong and burned out
- Never had a growth plan

Your job is to apply **quick, high-leverage fixes** that generate results fast — often in the first 30 days.

The Turnaround Triangle: Traffic – Monetization – Systems

Almost every underperforming business suffers in at least one of three areas:

1. Traffic (Attract)

- Outdated SEO (fix titles, update content)
- No social media or community sharing

- No email capture or lead magnets
- No paid ads or retargeting

Quick Wins:

- Use Ubersuggest to find missing keywords
- Add CTAs and lead magnets to high-traffic pages
- Launch 1–2 simple paid campaigns (Google/Meta/YouTube)

2. Monetization (Convert)

- No products, offers, or funnels
- Weak or expired affiliate links
- Poor pricing or lack of upsells

Quick Wins:

- Launch a $7–$27 digital product (checklists, templates, or mini-course)
- Add affiliate links and plug them into top pages or emails

- Use Stripe, Gumroad, or ThriveCart for fast checkout setup

3. Systems (Deliver & Scale)

- No automation or email follow-ups
- Manual processes for everything
- Broken tech, bad UX, or no analytics

Quick Wins:

- Add email automation with ConvertKit, MailerLite, or Beehiiv
- Set up Google Analytics & Hotjar for behavior insights
- Use Zapier or Make to automate lead capture, tagging, and CRM flows

When these three areas are aligned, the business runs smoother, makes more money, and can scale — **even with the same amount of traffic.**

The 30-Day Turnaround Blueprint

Here's a general timeline you can follow after acquisition:

Week 1: Audit & Fix

- Update broken links and pages
- Optimize top 10 traffic pages
- Fix slow load times or UX problems

Week 2: Monetization

- Add 1–2 affiliate links to popular content
- Launch or bundle a small offer
- Add checkout and email opt-in forms

Week 3: List Building & Automations

- Add exit popups or scroll boxes
- Build a 3–5 email nurture sequence
- Create one lead magnet (PDF, checklist, or video)

Week 4: Traffic Revival

- Refresh and republish older content
- Run a small paid ad test
- Post on Reddit, FB groups, or forums in your niche

Result: Most of these changes can **2–5x revenue and engagement** in just 30 days.

AI Tools That Accelerate Turnarounds

Speed is your secret weapon. Use AI to get more done in less time:

- **ChatGPT** – For rewriting content, generating offers, writing emails
- **Jasper** – For blog posts and social media automation
- **InVideo** – For faceless video creation and repurposing
- **Beehiiv** – For newsletter growth and automation
- **TidyCal** – To book calls if you add consulting services

If you're good at **orchestrating** — not necessarily doing everything — you can transform a failing business into a thriving one without burnout.

Positioning for a Future Exit

From the moment you take over a business, think like a future seller:

- Track every improvement (before/after screenshots, dashboards)

- Clean up finances (use Wave or QuickBooks)
- Write SOPs or Loom videos on operations
- Build a story around the turnaround

Buyers LOVE comeback stories – and you can often sell the same business for **3–10x more** once the numbers show growth and systems.

"The $1K Newsletter That Got a Second Life"

I once bought an old newsletter business for $1,000.

The seller had 1,800 subscribers but hadn't sent an email in 6 months. The domain was solid. The niche? Personal productivity.

I asked, "Why'd you stop?"

He said:

> "It was fun at first, but I got married, got a job, and ran out of ideas."

I paid him on the spot.

The first thing I did was clean up the list.

Only 1,200 emails were still valid. I imported them into Beehiiv, wrote a short reintroduction:

> "Hey, I'm Joe — I just bought this newsletter and I'm bringing it back. Want in?"

50% opened. 17% clicked. We were back.

The turnaround plan:

- Week 1: Cleaned up the branding, added a new logo with Canva
- Week 2: Added a productivity tool affiliate link to the welcome email
- Week 3: Wrote a 5-part automation series with ChatGPT and plugged in 2 low-ticket offers
- Week 4: Posted a free "Notion Template Bundle" on Product Hunt to drive signups

Result?

The list grew to 2,400 within 30 days. I was making $480/month from affiliate tools and templates. But then something amazing happened...

Someone reached out:

> "Hey, I run a productivity YouTube channel. Do you want to sell your list?"

We hopped on Zoom. He was relaunching a course and wanted warm leads.

I sold him the newsletter, including the archive, automations, and template funnel – for **$9,000.**

$1K in → 30 days of smart work → $480/month cash flow → $9K exit.

Here's the truth: You don't need to build from scratch to win online.

Sometimes, the best ROI is buried in the inbox of someone who gave up too early.

Chapter 5: Why You Have Leverage in Distressed Deals

When buying underperforming or distressed digital businesses, remember this:

You're solving a problem for the seller.

They're tired. They want to walk away. Many feel guilty or embarrassed that their business stalled — and just want a clean exit.

This puts *you* in a powerful position to negotiate:

- A **lower price**
- **Flexible payment terms**
- **Low upfront investment** (even $0 in some cases)
- **Risk-sharing agreements**

The key is to show them you're serious, not opportunistic. Be professional, but firm.

Framing the Offer Like a Pro

Instead of saying:

> "I'll give you $2,000."

Say this:

> "I'm excited about the potential here. Based on the current traffic and monetization gaps, I'd be comfortable offering $1,500 upfront, and I can close within 48 hours. We could also include a small earn-out if performance improves — let me know what works best for you."

This communicates:

- You've done your homework
- You understand the business
- You're giving them a fast, clean exit
- You're open to structuring it in their favor

Creative Structures for Smarter Deals

Distressed deals don't need to be all-cash. Here are common **low-risk structures**:

1. Low Cash + Earn-Out

> $1,500 upfront + $500/month for 3 months *if* revenue hits a target.

Great when:

- Revenue is inconsistent
- You need seller support for a bit

2. Seller Financing

$1,000 upfront + $250/month for 6 months.

This is like buying a business on layaway. It works if:

- Seller is reasonable
- You're confident you can boost cash flow quickly

3. Revenue Share Buyout

$0 upfront + 50% of profits for 6 months, then full transfer.

Use this when:

- You're taking over a dead or abandoned asset
- Seller just wants out but is unsure of the value

4. Asset-Only Purchase

Buy just the content, domain, or list.

This is powerful when:

- You don't want the tech headaches
- You just want traffic, emails, or branding

Due Diligence Clauses & Buyer Protection

No matter the structure, protect yourself. Add a **basic agreement** with:

Confirmation of asset ownership

Transfer of IP, access, and rights

Refund clause if seller misrepresented key metrics

Non-compete (for 1–2 years in the same niche)

Use tools like:

- **LegalZoom contract templates**
- **DocuSign** for signatures
- Or work with a low-cost lawyer via **UpCounsel** or **Fiverr Pro**

Knowing When to Walk Away

Even if the price is low, don't move forward if:

- The seller is sketchy or evasive
- The niche is a poor fit for your skills
- The core asset (domain, brand, or audience) has no real value
- The tech stack is too broken or custom

Trust your gut — and be ready to say **"Thanks, but I'll pass."**

There's always another deal.

"The SaaS Owner Who Just Wanted to Move On"

I once found a small SaaS tool on a niche forum.

It was a podcast episode generator — clean UI, basic features, and some loyal users. But the owner had gone silent. No updates in 8 months. No support. MRR was down to $180/month.

I emailed him.

> "Hey, I like what you built. Are you still running this?"

He replied:

> “Honestly, I’m done. I got hired at a startup. It’s just sitting there. I’d take $3K to hand it off.”

I didn’t jump at the number.

Instead, I scheduled a Zoom call and asked:

- What tech stack was it built on?
- Who owned the code?
- Did he have a Stripe or PayPal account still connected?

He said yes to all — and that he’d give me access before payment to test it out.

I reviewed everything, logged in, tested the generator, confirmed MRR, and ran a speed audit. It worked.

I offered this:

> "$1,000 upfront. $1,000 after 30 days if churn drops. 10% of all revenue for 6 months after that."

He paused.

> “Honestly, I’m fine with that if you can handle support and fixes.”

Deal.

We signed a basic Google Doc with IP transfer, passwords, and Stripe access.

What happened next?

- I added onboarding emails with ConvertKit
- I offered a $29/year annual plan (most switched from $5/month)
- I fixed one feature using a $200 developer from Upwork
- I got two YouTubers in the podcast niche to promote it

Within 60 days:

- MRR rose to $420
- Churn dropped
- He got his full $2K
- I was now earning $300+ passive income

The lesson?

You don't always need cash to buy a business. You need creativity, trust, and a good eye for opportunity.

And sometimes... A seller just wants peace of mind.

Chapter 6: Why Traffic Is the Lifeline of Your Turnaround

Fixing operations and monetization is key – but traffic is the **lifeblood** that drives long-term success. If you double traffic while improving conversions, you multiply revenue **exponentially**.

Distressed businesses usually have:

- Stale content
- No paid campaigns
- No audience engagement strategy

Fortunately, that's your edge.

The Two-Traffic Engine: Organic + Paid

Think of your growth as a two-engine system:

Engine 1: Organic Traffic

This includes:

- SEO (Search engine optimization)
- YouTube and blog content

- Email list growth
- Social media posts
- Product Hunt or Reddit features

Engine 2: Paid Traffic

This includes:

- Google Search Ads (high intent)
- YouTube Ads (great for info products or courses)
- Facebook/Instagram Ads (retargeting, lead gen)
- Reddit Ads (for niche communities)
- Sponsored newsletters or shoutouts

Most underperforming businesses rely on **neither**. That's your opportunity.

Simple Organic Growth Strategies That Work

Even if you don't have SEO or content experience, start here:

Update Existing Content

- Use **ChatGPT or Surfer SEO** to re-optimize headlines and structure

- Add FAQs and internal links
- Repost to Quora, Medium, and LinkedIn

Publish Quick Wins

- 500–800 word posts using long-tail keywords
- Focus on “how to,” “best tools,” “templates,” or “alternatives” searches
- Use **Ubersuggest** for ideas

Build Topical Authority

- Create mini-content clusters (3–5 articles around one theme)
- Example: “How to Get a Mortgage” → Article 1: Credit Score Tips, Article 2: Income Docs, Article 3: Mistakes to Avoid

Capture Emails with Lead Magnets

- Add a popup or inline opt-in to your highest traffic pages
- Offer a 1-page PDF, checklist, or template

Paid Ads: Low-Cost, High-Control Growth

Once you know your funnel works, paid traffic can scale your results fast. Start small:

Google Ads

- Run keyword-targeted search ads
- Use "exact match" or "phrase match" to avoid wasted spend
- Send traffic to a lead capture page or low-ticket product

YouTube Ads

- Target by keyword, channel, or topic
- Use 60–90 second ads (try faceless or AI voice if needed)
- Promote free lead magnet or low-cost bundle

Meta (Facebook/Instagram)

- Start with retargeting: site visitors, email opens, or cart abandoners
- Test creative using video reels, testimonials, or story-style hooks

Start with **$5–$15/day** and scale only when your ROI is proven.

Audience Borrowing: Grow Using Other People's Traffic

When organic and paid traffic are slow or expensive, **borrow audiences**. This is especially powerful with niche underperforming businesses.

Tactics:

- Partner with **micro-influencers** (YouTubers, podcasters, IG creators)
- Pitch guest blog posts or newsletter swaps
- Comment and engage in **Facebook Groups, Reddit, Discord**
- Launch your turnaround story on IndieHackers or Product Hunt

You can often get **hundreds of visits/day** just by tapping into the right niche audiences without spending a dime.

Compound Traffic = Predictable Growth

The best part? These efforts compound.

- SEO traffic grows month over month

- Emails build trust over time
- Paid traffic becomes cheaper as you optimize
- Community engagement drives word-of-mouth

Even a distressed business with only 1,000 visits/month can grow to **10,000+** in under 90 days with consistent effort — especially if the foundation is solid.

“Turning an Abandoned Blog into a Traffic Machine”

When I bought the blog, it was barely alive.

- 3,200 monthly visits (mostly from one article)
- No new posts in 18 months
- No email list
- $0 revenue

But the domain had history. The niche (budget travel) was solid. And the article getting traffic was titled:

> “How to Fly to Europe for Under $300.”

I didn't change everything. I just **focused on what was already working.**

My 30-Day Plan

Week 1:

- Updated the Europe travel article with better structure, keywords, and an embedded CTA
- Used ChatGPT to rewrite it in 3 formats: blog, newsletter, and LinkedIn post
- Added a lead magnet: "Cheap Flight Alerts Tracker" (Google Sheet + 5 email tips)

Week 2:

- Published 2 more posts: "How I Got to Mexico for $98" and "Best Credit Cards for Flights"
- Joined 3 Reddit threads and posted helpful answers linking back to my article
- Signed up for an affiliate program for travel cards and insurance

Week 3:

- Ran a $10/day Facebook ad to the lead magnet with a free trip-planning template
- Launched a weekly "Budget Travel Friday" newsletter
- Hit 500 email subscribers by day 21

Week 4:

- Reached out to a popular YouTuber with 15K subs and offered him a free Notion planner to feature
- He plugged my link in his description → traffic doubled overnight

60 Days Later:

- Traffic: 3,200 → 11,000 visits/month
- Email List: 0 → 1,800 subscribers
- Monthly Revenue: $0 → $710 (affiliate + trip planner bundle)
- Site Valuation: 3–5x higher than purchase price

And I was only working on it **5 hours/week**.

The best part?

That growth didn't come from genius – just **consistency, clarity, and low-cost traffic strategies**.

I didn't build an empire. I revived one — and made it better.

Chapter 7: Why Systems Are the Difference Between a Job and an Asset

Most people think the hardest part of buying a business is the turnaround. But the real wealth is built in what comes *after* that:

Automating. Delegating. Scaling.

Without systems, you're just replacing the old owner — and inheriting their burnout. With systems, the business becomes an **asset** — one that grows whether or not you show up.

The Three Levels of Automation

Here's how to think about system-building after you've taken over:

Level 1: Self

- Streamline your own workflow
- Use SOPs (standard operating procedures)
- Save logins in a secure password manager (1Password, LastPass)
- Create a "Daily/Weekly Checklist" to guide your activity

Level 2: Software

- Use automation tools to eliminate repetitive tasks
- Examples:
    - **Zapier/Make** – Automate lead capture, CRM tagging, file delivery
    - **ConvertKit/MailerLite** – Automate email sequences, tagging, and list cleaning
    - **Gumroad/ThriveCart** – Automate checkout, upsells, and delivery

Level 3: Staff or Freelancers

- Delegate tasks to low-cost VAs
- Start with:
    - Content scheduling
    - Email replies
    - Customer support
    - Updating blog posts
    - Simple video edits

Train them once — let them handle the repetition forever.

The 5 Foundational Systems You Need

Every online business, no matter how small, should have these five core systems in place:

1. Traffic System

- Weekly SEO audit + update checklist
- Blog/video content calendar
- Ad campaign templates

2. Lead Capture System

- Opt-in forms on top pages
- Automated welcome series
- Lead magnet delivery

3. Monetization System

- Sales page with upsell/downsell options
- Email campaigns for promotions
- Affiliate product tracking

4. Fulfillment & Delivery

- Automated digital delivery (PDFs, templates, login info)
- Thank you page with upsell or community invite
- Instant access emails

5. Support & Feedback

- Help desk or simple support form
- Response templates for FAQs
- Automated feedback request after purchase

Tools to Build and Run These Systems

You don't need a massive tech stack. These tools are beginner-friendly and scale well:

Function	Tools
Email Marketing	ConvertKit, MailerLite, Beehiiv
Payments & Delivery	Stripe, Gumroad, ThriveCart
CRM & Automation	Notion, Airtable, Zapier
Website	Carrd, WordPress, Webflow
SOPs & Training	Loom (video), Scribe (click-tracking), Google Docs

If the business already uses one of these – keep it. Don't reinvent unless necessary.

Scaling: One Product, Many Platforms

Once your systems are in place, it's time to **multiply** reach and revenue:

- Repurpose content into **YouTube Shorts, IG Reels, TikToks**
- Convert blog posts into **a free ebook** to collect leads
- Bundle your product and list it on:
    - AppSumo
    - Gumroad Marketplace
    - Etsy (if it's templates/tools)
    - Udemy (if it's a course)
- Use your SOPs to launch **a second or third product quickly**

Now, you're no longer just fixing a business. You're **building a scalable brand** with automated momentum.

"From Overwhelmed to Outsourced: My First Fully Systemized Business"

I bought a meal prep blog in 2023 for $1,800.

It had:

- 7,000 monthly visits

- A basic $17 PDF meal plan
- 3 years of untouched content
- A tired creator who said:

  "I just can't do this anymore. I have two kids and zero time."

I thought: *Perfect.*

At first, I tried to do it all myself — updating content, answering emails, managing coupons. Within 10 days, I realized I had made a mistake.

The blog didn't need *me*. It needed **systems**.

So I stopped trying to be the hero — and became the builder.

Week 1: Setup

- Created a Notion dashboard with:
- Content checklist
- Weekly email calendar
- Monthly analytics tracker
- Built a welcome email sequence in ConvertKit

- Installed ThriveCart for cleaner checkout and upsell delivery

Week 2: Delegate

- Hired a VA from the Philippines at $7/hr
- Trained her via Loom videos to:
- Schedule posts
- Reply to email questions
- Clean the email list weekly
- Gave her a simple rulebook:

“If it’s not in the SOP, ask me once. Then make it better next time.”

Week 3: Scale

- Launched a second PDF: “Vegetarian Meal Prep for Busy Moms”
- Created a bundle with both guides for $27
- Ran a $10/day FB ad targeting parenting groups
- Used Zapier to:

- Tag users by product
- Trigger upsell emails
- Deliver the bonus content automatically

By week 5, I barely touched the business.

3 Months Later:

- Revenue: $400 → $1,600/month
- Hours worked: 20/month → 3/month
- Tasks: 90% handled by automation or my VA
- Value of business: now worth $12K+ on Flippa

I didn't build a content empire. I built a **machine.**

Now when I look at businesses to buy, I ask:

> "Can I automate this in under 30 days?"

If yes — it's a yes.

Chapter 8: Know Your Endgame Before You Begin

Every turnaround should start with one key question:

"Am I building this to flip or to keep?"

There's no wrong answer. But your **strategy changes** depending on your goal:

- **Flip:** Focus on speed, visual improvements, and monthly revenue growth
- **Hold:** Focus on systems, brand assets, and stability over time

Distressed businesses can be ideal for either strategy – **but not both at once**. Choose your path.

Key Metrics Buyers Look For (If You Want to Sell)

If your endgame is an exit, understand what makes your business *attractive* to buyers:

Metric	**Ideal Target**
Monthly Net Profit	Consistent or growing (90-day average)
Traffic	Stable or increasing (esp. organic)
Churn	Low for SaaS or memberships (<5–8%)
Email List	Active with decent open/click rates
SOPs	Clear processes documented
Owner Involvement	Under 5–10 hours/week is ideal
Tech Stack	Simple and transferable

The **easier** it is for the buyer to take over and grow it, the **higher the multiple** they'll pay.

Increase Your Exit Multiple: Value Add Strategies

Most online businesses sell for **1.5x to 3.5x monthly net profit**, depending on size, risk, and automation.

Want to push your valuation higher?

Do these before listing:

- Add a second revenue stream (ads + affiliate, or product + coaching)
- Automate fulfillment and support
- Reduce churn or refund rates
- Create visual dashboards (Notion, Airtable, or Google Sheets)
- Write SOPs for everything — content, marketing, fulfillment

Document your **turnaround story** — buyers love “from broken to profitable” case studies.

Where to Sell for Maximum Value

Depending on your business type and price point, use the right platform:

Platform	Best For
Flippa	<$50K deals, content sites, beginners
Acquire.com	SaaS and productized services ($25K–$500K)
Empire Flippers	$50K+ deals with vetted numbers
FE International	High-end SaaS and ecom ($100K–$10M)
Private Network	Personal brand, micro-acquisitions (email lists, newsletters, assets)

Also consider:

- Posting to **IndieHackers**, **Reddit**, or **niche Slack groups**
- Emailing previous buyers from past deals
- Using brokers only **if** you're targeting a higher valuation (they'll take a 10–15% cut)

Long-Term Hold Playbook: Build a Cash-Flowing Mini Empire

If you choose to **hold**, your job becomes about efficiency, asset stacking, and low-maintenance growth:

Monthly Checklist for Held Businesses:

- Review traffic + sales performance
- Optimize top 10 content pieces
- Review ad campaigns or email flows
- Assign content/tasks to VAs
- Repurpose one asset (video → blog, blog → social)

After 90 days of solid automation, consider **buying a second or third business** in a complementary niche.

You can:

- Cross-promote products
- Share email lists
- Share your VA team
- Bundle assets for a future mega-exit

That's how you go from a single flip... to a **portfolio worth six or seven figures.**

"The Email List That Became a Six-Figure Exit"

I never planned to sell it.

It started with a $2,700 newsletter acquisition: 3,000 subscribers, slow growth, a couple of dead links. The niche? Remote work and digital productivity.

I revived it like I had with others:

- Sent out a reintroduction email
- Offered a free Trello template
- Launched a $27 product bundle for freelancers

Within 6 months, I had:

- 8,900 subscribers
- 38% open rates
- $1,100/month recurring income from products + affiliate deals

But then something interesting happened.

A buyer from a previous deal reached out:

> "Hey, are you the one running Remote Pro Weekly? I love it. Ever think about selling?"

At first, I said no. But I asked him what he had in mind.

He replied:

> "I'd offer $42,000 if you can show stable numbers and transfer the assets cleanly."

I wasn't expecting that — but I was prepared.

I sent:

- Screenshots of Stripe, ConvertKit, and Gumroad
- My Notion dashboard with all SOPs
- A Loom walkthrough of operations
- A signed non-compete

He said: "Let's do it." We closed within 2 weeks. I had just turned a $2.7K investment into **$42K** — while collecting passive income the whole time.

Now I always build with the exit in mind.

Whether I sell or not, I act like I might. Because a clean, systemized, growing business is always:

- Easier to run

- More valuable

- And far more *fun* to own

Chapter 9: From a Single Deal to a Portfolio of Profit Machines

Once you've turned around your first business – and proven the process works – the next logical step is:

Repeat. Systemize. Scale.

Distressed online businesses aren't just one-time opportunities. They're a blueprint for long-term wealth. If you build with intention, you can turn one $2K flip into a **portfolio of cash-flowing assets** worth six figures or more.

The Portfolio Mindset: Act Like a Mini PE Firm

Professional investors build portfolios of underperforming companies, improve them, and either:

- Hold them for stable cash flow, or
- Exit when multiples are high

You can do the same. You don't need millions in capital. You just need:

- A repeatable process
- A low-cost team or toolset

- Clarity on your time and exit strategy

Treat yourself like a **mini private equity firm**. Your business is to buy **digital real estate**, renovate it, and turn it into a profit center.

How to Structure Your Portfolio Growth

Start simple:

Phase 1 – Learn & Prove (Deal 1)

- Invest <$5K
- Do the turnaround yourself
- Learn the process, tools, and common problems

Phase 2 – Repeat with Systems (Deals 2–3)

- Use cash flow from Deal 1 to fund Deal 2
- Build SOPs from your first experience
- Hire a part-time VA or freelancer
- Add more automation to scale

Phase 3 – Stack & Diversify (Deals 4–6+)

- Buy businesses in **complementary niches**

- Build central systems: one email platform, one project tracker
- Create bundles or cross-promotions
- Begin grooming one business for a larger exit

Now you're no longer a buyer. You're an operator of a **digital asset portfolio**.

Reducing Burnout While Scaling

Scaling doesn't mean doing more — it means **delegating better**.

Here's how to stay lean:

- Use one VA across all businesses (with clear roles)
- Use automation tools to unify lead capture, product delivery, and analytics
- Schedule one "strategy day" per week to work *on* the business, not *in* it
- Keep all SOPs, passwords, and analytics in **one Notion or Airtable hub**

You should be spending <10 hours/week managing 3+ assets once systems are live.

Exit or Hold: Designing Your Endgame

Every 90 days, ask yourself:

> "Do I want to flip this business or keep it as a cash-flowing machine?"

You can:

- **Flip low-effort businesses** to build capital
- **Hold high-margin businesses** with great systems
- **Bundle multiple sites** for a larger sale (this increases your valuation multiple)

A business worth $10K solo might be worth $50K+ as part of a **bundle sale**.

Keep clean books, document everything, and track KPIs for each property.

You're not just a side hustler anymore — you're building a **digital empire**.

"From $1,000 to $150,000 — The Portfolio That Paid for My Freedom"

It started with one little blog.

I bought it for $1,000. Fixed a few pages. Added email automation. Ran a $5/day ad. It made back its cost in 3 weeks.

I sold it 3 months later for $5,500. That was my "aha" moment.

So I repeated the process.

- Deal 2: A neglected finance course website
- Paid: $3,300
- Added a $47 upsell
- Result: $1,200/month in passive sales

Kept it.

Deal 3: A micro SaaS Chrome extension for freelancers

- Paid: $2,000
- Revenue: $140/month
- Fixed onboarding
- Added yearly plan
- Now: $480/month MRR

Kept that too.

By month 12, I had:

- 5 businesses
- 4 VAs
- A Notion board with SOPs for everything
- $4,200/month in semi-passive income

I wasn't rich — but I was **free**. I stopped freelancing. I traveled. I bought a new laptop and moved into a place I actually liked.

The big win? I sold 3 of the businesses together as a bundle — blog + newsletter + course site — for **$83,000**.

The buyer was thrilled to get a systemized mini-brand. I was thrilled to **cash out and reinvest.**

Today, I own 8 properties. Most require less than 5 hours/month. Combined, they generate:

- $8K–$10K/month profit
- With 3 more scheduled for exit next year

All from distressed businesses no one else wanted.

Final lesson?

You don't need to build the next Amazon. You just need to fix what others forgot about — and turn messes into machines.

Closing Thoughts

You've now learned the complete process of turning neglected online businesses into profitable digital assets.

Let's recap what you've unlocked:

- **How to spot undervalued businesses** that others overlook
- **Where to find them**, even off-market
- **How to analyze traffic, revenue, and systems** like a pro
- **Tactical turnarounds** that create 2–5x growth in 30–90 days
- **Deal structuring strategies** that require little to no upfront cash
- **Automation frameworks** that remove you from day-to-day operations
- And how to **scale your efforts into a full portfolio** — one that provides real cash flow, freedom, and long-term value

This isn't theory. It's a repeatable business model.

Final Words from the Author

I started this journey with a single low-budget blog that no one wanted.

No team. No fancy office. No startup capital. Just strategy, resourcefulness, and consistent action.

That first deal changed everything — not because it made me rich, but because it proved this:

Opportunity lives in neglected corners. And if you know how to spot it... You can turn digital dust into gold.

Whether you plan to flip, hold, or bundle your way to financial independence, this book was created to help you shortcut the trial-and-error — and act with confidence.

www.ingramcontent.com/pod-product-compliance
Lightning Source LLC
LaVergne TN
LVHW022022200926
848481LV00007B/2485